Yukon

Yukon

Lyn Hancock

Fitzhenry & Whiteside

Lerner website address: www.lernerbooks.com

Licensed to Fitzhenry & Whiteside for exclusive sale in Canada by arrangement with the Lerner Publishing Group

Fitzhenry & Whiteside
195 Allstate Parkway
Markham, ON L3R 4T8

Canadian Cataloguing in Publication

Hancock, Lyn, 1938–
   Yukon
(Hello Canada)
Includes index.
ISBN 1–55041–263–9
1. Yukon Territory—Juvenile literature. I. Title. II. Series.
FC4011.2.H36 1998   j971.9'1   C98–930929–0
F1091.4.H36 1998

Manufactured in the United States of America
2 3 4 5 6 7 – JR – 03 02 01 00 99 98

VILLE DE MONTREAL

3 2777 0219 8730 5

Cover photograph by Lyn Hancock. Background photo by R. Chen / SuperStock.

The glossary that starts on page 68 gives definitions of words shown in **bold type** in the text.

Senior Editor
Gretchen Bratvold
Editors
Lori Coleman
Domenica Di Piazza
Photo Researcher
Cindy Hartmon Nelson
Series Designer
Steve Foley
Designer
Mike Tacheny

Our thanks to Dawson City historian John Gould and to author, journalist, and publisher Florence Whyard for their help in preparing this book.

This book is printed on acid-free, recyclable paper.

Contents

Fun Facts

🍁 Every September contestants in the Great Klondike Outhouse Race dash through downtown Dawson City, Yukon. Teams consist of five people—four runners pushing an outhouse on wheels with one person sitting inside.

🍁 The largest gold nugget ever discovered in North America was found near Haines Junction in southern Yukon in the 1980s. The nugget weighed 9 pounds (4.1 kilograms).

🍁 The world's largest weather vane is located at the airport in Whitehorse, Yukon. The instrument—which shows the direction of the wind—is made from an airplane mounted on a rotating pedestal.

Hi! My name is Barkley. As you read *Yukon*, I will be helping you make sense of some of the maps and charts that appear in the book.

People who visit Watson Lake, Yukon, still plaster the names of their hometowns in the Signpost Forest.

Carl Lindley, a homesick Alaska Highway construction worker, planted a signpost at Watson Lake, Yukon, in 1942. The sign listed the mileage to his hometown of Danville, Illinois. People from all over the world have added more than 20,000 signs to what is now known as the Signpost Forest.

The Spell of the Yukon

It's the great, big, broad land 'way up yonder,
It's the forest where silence has lease,
It's the beauty that thrills me with wonder,
It's the stillness that fills me with peace.

(from "The Spell of the Yukon" by Robert Service)

Yukoners as well as outsiders are drawn to the Yukon Territory by magnificent scenery, romantic history, friendly people, and the promise of freedom and adventure in a remote wilderness. A little larger than the U.S. state of California, the Yukon Territory is a pie-shaped wedge in the northwestern corner of Canada.

Moose

The Yukon—one of Canada's three territories—is squeezed between the Northwest Territories on the east and the U.S. state of Alaska on the west. British Columbia lies to the south, while the icy waters of the Beaufort Sea (an arm of the Arctic Ocean) form the Yukon's northern shoreline.

Almost everywhere in the Yukon are long chains of rugged mountains divided by **plateaus,** or flat highlands, and deep valleys. This landscape is part of the **Cordillera,** a belt of mountainous terrain that stretches along the entire western edge of North and South America.

The Yukon's landscape was formed over the last billion years, as enormous sections of the earth's crust collided with one another. These forces caused the land to lift, buckle, and fold, creating mountains and wedging mineral deposits between layers of rock. Wind, water, and **glaciers** (huge, slow-moving sheets of ice) further shaped the territory's landscape.

The Yukon is divided into four regions—the Western Cordillera, the Interior Plateau, the Eastern Cordillera, and the Arctic Coastal Plain. The Saint Elias Range and the Coast Mountains stretch across the Western Cordillera, which covers the southwestern corner of the Yukon. These mountains contain some of the tallest peaks in North America. Massive Mount Logan, in the Saint Elias Range, is the highest mountain in Canada and the second highest in North America.

Mount Logan rises 19,550 feet (5,959 meters) in the Saint Elias Range.

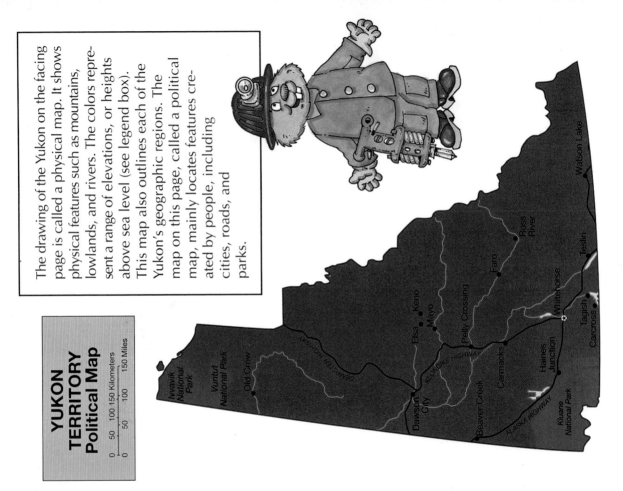

The drawing of the Yukon on the facing page is called a physical map. It shows physical features such as mountains, lowlands, and rivers. The colors represent a range of elevations, or heights above sea level (see legend box). This map also outlines each of the Yukon's geographic regions. The map on this page, called a political map, mainly locates features created by people, including cities, roads, and parks.

YUKON TERRITORY Political Map

0 50 100 150 Kilometers
0 50 100 150 Miles

Ivvavik National Park

Vuntut National Park

Old Crow

DEMPSTER HIGHWAY

Dawson City

Beaver Creek

ALASKA HIGHWAY

Kluane National Park

Elsa • Keno
Mayo

Faro

Ross River

Pelly Crossing

KLONDIKE HIGHWAY

Carmacks

Haines Junction

Whitehorse

Teslin

Tagish

Carcross

Watson Lake

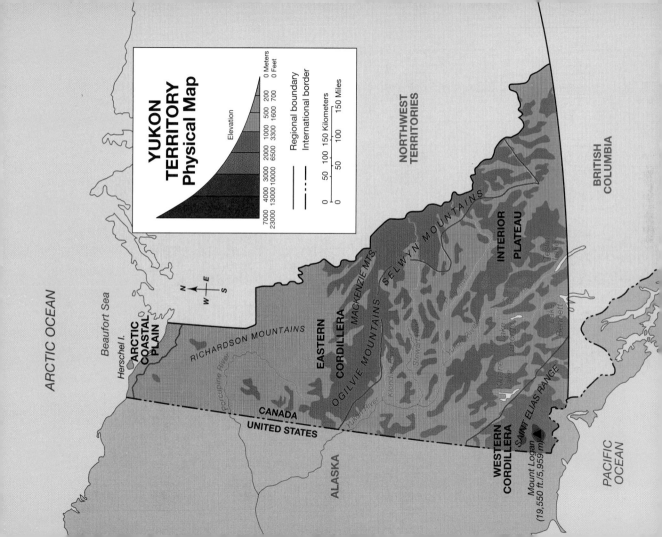

YUKON TERRITORY Physical Map

Elevation

Meters	Feet
0	0
200	700
500	1600
1000	3300
2000	6500
3000	10000
4000	13000
7000	23000

Regional boundary
International border

150 Kilometers 100 50 0
150 Miles 100 50 0

N
E
W
S

ARCTIC OCEAN

Beaufort Sea

Herschel I.

ARCTIC COASTAL PLAIN

RICHARDSON MOUNTAINS

Porcupine River

CANADA
UNITED STATES

ALASKA

Yukon River

PACIFIC OCEAN

WESTERN CORDILLERA

SAINT ELIAS RANGE

Mount Logan
(19,550 ft./5,959 m)

EASTERN CORDILLERA

OGILVIE MOUNTAINS

MACKENZIE MTS.

SELWYN MOUNTAINS

INTERIOR PLATEAU

Klondike River

Stewart River

Lake Laberge

Kluane Lake

Lake Bennett

NORTHWEST TERRITORIES

BRITISH COLUMBIA

A glacier plows down a slope in the Saint Elias Range. The glacier is part of an enormous ice field that is believed to be at least 2,297 feet (700 m) thick in some places.

The Saint Elias Range also holds the world's largest fields of permanent ice and snow located outside of the earth's polar regions. Some of the ice is left over from the most recent **Ice Age,** which ended about 10,000 years ago.

Pockets of permanent ice also remain in high valleys and on north-facing slopes in the Eastern Cordillera. The main ranges in this region are the Ogilvie, the Richardson, the Selwyn, and the Mackenzie Mountains. The mountains in the Eastern Cordillera are older and not as rugged as those in the Western Cordillera.

The weatherworn Ogilvie Mountains (left) *stretch across the Eastern Cordillera. Tutshi Lake* (below) *lies in the southern Interior Plateau.*

In between the Cordillera regions lie the smaller mountains, plateaus, and deep valleys of the Interior Plateau. The western half of this region is one of the few places in Canada that wasn't covered by glaciers during the last Ice Age.

The mighty Yukon River, the second longest river in Canada, flows through the Interior Plateau. Other large waterways in the Yukon—including the Teslin, Pelly, Stewart, Porcupine, and Klondike Rivers—feed the Yukon River.

In the 1800s, British trader John Bell called the river Youcon, after a Gwich'in Indian name meaning "great river." The spelling eventually changed to Yukon, which became the official name for both the river and the territory.

The Yukon River (left) *crosses about 2,000 miles (3,218 kilometers) on its way from the Yukon-British Columbia border to the Bering Sea. Bearberries, crowberries, and lichens* (facing page, right) *are some of the hardy plants that grow on the Arctic Coastal Plain in northern Yukon.*

A Land Where Mountains Are Nameless

Robert Service, a famous poet born in England in 1874, spent eight years in the Yukon and wrote many famous verses about the northern land he loved. Service called the Yukon "a land where mountains are nameless," but the Aboriginal peoples in the territory already had their own names for the Yukon's geographical features. For example, the Tagish people of southern Yukon knew Fourth of July Mountain as Médzíh Dzéle', which means "caribou mountain." In the Tlingit language, the foot trail between Tagish and Carcross is called Xóots Leitu<u>x</u>ká, which means "bear windpipe." Alligator Lake, south of Whitehorse, is called Jekudìtl'eda, which means "where ice breaks up (and grayling come through)" in the language of the Southern Tutchone.

Besides mountains, the Yukon also has lowlands. Sprinkled with lakes and ponds, the flat Arctic Coastal Plain lies along the Arctic coast in northern Yukon. Called **permafrost,** the ground in this region is permanently frozen. Only a thin layer of surface soil thaws each year, allowing mosses, lichens, and low-growing trees—such as dwarf willows, dwarf birches, and Labrador teas—to grow.

17

Once inhabited by Aboriginal peoples, Herschel Island became a whaling station in the 1800s and a military post in the 1900s. Since the 1960s, this island off the Yukon's Arctic coast has had no permanent residents.

Just one mile (1.6 kilometers) off the Arctic coast is Herschel Island. Flat and treeless, the island is home to a variety of plants and animals, including polar bears and arctic foxes.

In general, the Yukon's climate is cold. This is partly because the territory's high mountains block warm Pacific winds from blowing into the region. In addition, the Yukon straddles the Arctic Circle, an imaginary map line that marks the southern boundary of the frigid Arctic region.

In winter, areas close to the Arctic Circle receive almost no sunshine. But during the short summers, they receive almost continuous light. Along the Arctic coast, the sun never sets between the end of May and the middle of July. For this reason, the Yukon—like other northern regions—is often called Land of the Midnight Sun.

Summers in the territory are warm. In July residents of Whitehorse in southern Yukon enjoy average temperatures of about 57° F (14° C). Winters in the Yukon are long and cold. The average January temperature in Whitehorse is –5° F (–21° C). Farther north in Old Crow, average winter temperatures drop to –31° F (–35° C).

The Yukon is extremely dry year-round. Mountains block most of the moisture-carrying winds from the Pacific Ocean. For this reason, the territory receives only about 13 inches (33 centimeters) of **precipitation** (rain and snow) each year. Dry air cracks people's lips but makes winter seem less cold.

Winters in the Yukon usually last from September to June. The coldest temperature ever registered in the territory was –81° F (–63° C), recorded in Snag, Yukon, in 1947.

Because the territory is so dry and cold, only about 16 percent of the land is forested. Spruces, pines, firs, birches, poplars, and aspens are the main trees that can survive in the Yukon. But the territory is rich in wildflowers. Tall, pink fireweeds brighten roadsides in summer. The territory's many other flowers include mountain avens, arctic poppies, wild roses, lupines, and several types of wild orchids.

Wherever you go in the Yukon, you'll find animals. Black bears lick berries from forest floors. Grizzly bears

The Carcross Desert (facing page) *in southern Yukon is known as the world's smallest desert. Foxtail barley* (facing page, inset) *grows in other dry areas of the Yukon. A lynx* (below) *uses a fallen tree for a lookout post.*

dig in burrows looking for ground squirrels. Lynx pounce on snowshoe hares, while wolves chase moose along lakeshores. Dall sheep and mountain goats scale rocky mountain peaks. The territory's Arctic waters are home to beluga whales, walruses, and seals. Birds in the Yukon include eagles, hawks, gyrfalcons, loons, geese, ducks, and ravens.

Aboriginal (Native or First Nations) peoples depend on moose and caribou for meat and materials to make clothing. Like hunting, fishing is also important to Yukoners. The most popular fish are lake trout, arctic grayling, northern pike, Dolly Varden, and salmon. The prized arctic char of the Arctic coast lays eggs in the Firth River. Yes, there are many reasons why Yukoners love their land!

The First Peoples

Different groups have different ways of telling how the Yukon began and how people came to live in the region. Tales from the Tagish First Nation—a people of southern Yukon—say that in the beginning, there were just animals. Sea Lion owned the only land—an island. The rest of the world was water.

Crow stole Sea Lion's baby and refused to give it back until Sea Lion gave him sand, which Crow sprinkled over the water to create the world. Then, because Crow was lonely, he carved Man and Woman from poplar tree bark and breathed life into them.

Scientists believe that during the last Ice Age, Asia and North America were joined together in a huge northern land mass called Beringia. The area was home to many different animals, including woolly mammoths, giant beavers, lions, and camels.

Beringia was a good place to hunt, and people from Asia followed the animals across the region. Some of these hunters eventually came to what is now the Yukon. Scientists have found stone tools and animal bones near Old Crow, Yukon, that are at least 12,000 years old.

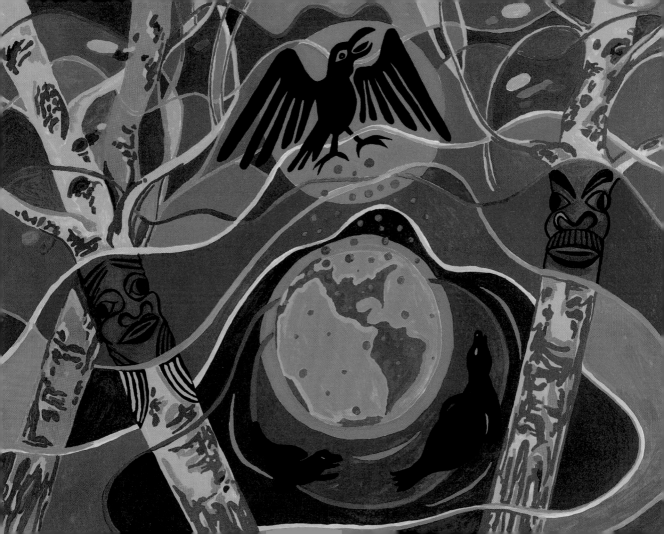

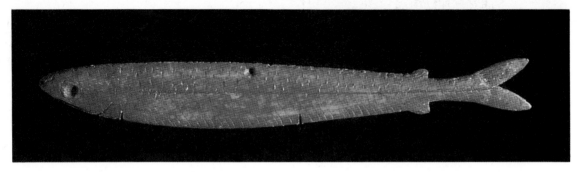

First Nations peoples in northern Yukon made this bone carving—probably a fishing lure—about 500 B.C.

Over time, many different Aboriginal groups settled in what is now the Yukon. These peoples are often grouped together according to the languages they spoke. For example, the Gwich'in, the Han, the Northern Tutchone, the Southern Tutchone, the Kaska, the Upper Tanana, and the Tagish all originally spoke Na-Dene (Athapascan) languages.

The Inland Tlingit people, who spoke Tlingit, came to the southern Yukon from what is now Alaska. The Inuvialuit, whose language is known as Inuvialuktun, lived along the Yukon's Arctic coast and on Herschel Island before moving east to the Northwest Territories in the early 1900s.

Aboriginals in the Yukon lived off the land. They fished, hunted, and

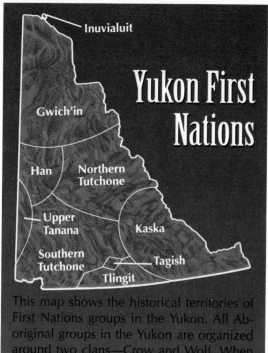

Yukon First Nations

Inuvialuit

Gwich'in

Han

Northern Tutchone

Upper Tanana

Kaska

Southern Tutchone

Tagish

Tlingit

This map shows the historical territories of First Nations groups in the Yukon. All Aboriginal groups in the Yukon are organized around two clans—Crow and Wolf. When children are born, they belong to their mother's clan. But when they marry, they must marry someone from the opposite clan. This ensures that ties are strong between the clans and between peoples from distant places.

gathered food according to the season. The people walked across their territory, camping wherever animals were plentiful. On land, Aboriginals carried belongings on their backs or dragged them on animal skins. On water, they relied on log rafts, birchbark canoes, or moose-hide boats.

While traveling, families lived in simple pole dwellings covered with brush. When they stayed in one place for a longer stretch of time, they built dome-shaped houses from poles and moss and covered the structures with moose or caribou skins.

In spring, hunters trapped beavers and muskrat and caught fish and birds. In summer, families gathered in camps along lakes and rivers to trap salmon, snare rabbits and gophers, and pick berries and other edible plants.

Summer was also the time for trading. In the north, the Gwich'in traded muskrat and wolverine furs for walrus hides and ivory tusks gathered by the Inuvialuit. The Tlingit came from what is now Alaska to trade fish oil, seaweed, dried clams, seashells, and cedar boxes for furs, moose-skin clothing, snowshoes, dyes, and mountain-goat hair.

In fall the people in what is now the Yukon went into the mountains to hunt sheep and caribou. When winter came, families fished through holes

Gwich'in dancers move to the beat of a ceremonial drum.

in the ice, trapped small animals, and ate the meat and fish they had dried earlier in the year.

Aboriginals in the Yukon survived for thousands of years in the region's harsh landscape. Each season they took only what they needed from the land. This lifeway began to change in the early 1800s, when European explorers first came to the territory. In 1825 British explorer and mapper John Franklin reached the Yukon's Arctic shores. In 1842 fur trader Robert Campbell built a trading post called Fort Frances for the Hudson's Bay Company, a British fur-trading empire.

Six years later, Campbell built Fort Selkirk on the Yukon River. Athapascan groups brought furs and food to these posts, where they traded for blankets, tobacco, guns, kettles, and beads.

Early fur trappers and traders often traveled through uncharted wilderness to reach trading posts, which were few and far between.

But the Tlingit, who had traded with the Athapascans for many years, grew angry over losing their trading partners. In 1852 the Tlingit burned down Fort Selkirk, which was not rebuilt for many years.

Newcomers from other parts of North America and from Europe slowly trickled into the region. Some came to open their own fur-trading posts. Beginning in the 1860s, European **missionaries** built schools and churches in what is now the Yukon. The missionaries taught the Christian religion and European lifeways to local Aboriginals. In the process of learning new ways, many Aboriginal children lost their traditional customs, languages, and religions.

Starting in the 1880s, U.S. whalers began coming to Herschel Island to

Young Inuvialuit girls (above) *at Akulurak, Yukon, prepare for their first communion, a Christian religious ceremony.*

hunt whales. At that time, whale oil was used to make fuel for streetlamps

Whalers struggle to keep their boat from capsizing on a large wave. The threat of falling into the icy Arctic waters off Herschel Island made whaling there especially dangerous.

in U.S. and Canadian cities. Baleen—a flexible material from the mouths of whales—was fashioned into fishing rods and reinforcements for women's corsets (undergarments).

The whalers also traded liquor, clothing, and other manufactured goods with the Inuvialuit for meat and furs. Many of the Aboriginals died from measles and other diseases that were unintentionally passed on by the newcomers.

Interest in the Yukon continued to grow in the late 1800s. In 1895 the Canadian government established the Yukon as an official district of the North-West Territories, a vast region of northwestern Canada. The government then sent the North-West Mounted Police to keep law and order in the area.

The next year, George Carmack, his Tagish wife, Kate, and her relatives Skookum Jim Mason and Dawson Charlie made an important discovery. They found big nuggets of gold in Bonanza Creek, near where the Klondike River meets the Yukon River in western Yukon. Soon, thousands of people from all over the world started a stampede for the remote Yukon, hoping to find gold and get rich.

Most Stampeders traveled to the Yukon by taking a boat up the Pacific coast to the towns of Skagway and Dyea in southeastern Alaska. Then they crossed the Coast Mountains through the Chilkoot Pass or the White Pass to Lake Bennett on the Yukon side.

Canada and the United States disagreed at this time about where the

WHO FOUND

One of the problems with history is that people remember events differently. For example, George Carmack claimed he was the first person to discover the gold that led to the Klondike Gold Rush. Carmack did indeed stake the discovery claim, but Skookum Jim said that *he* was the one who found the gold while Carmack was sleeping under a tree. Skookum Jim said the prospectors decided Carmack should stake the claim since they thought the government wouldn't allow an Aboriginal to do so.

Many non-Aboriginals have written about the gold rush, describing Skookum Jim as a strong packer. He could carry 156 pounds (71 kilograms) over the Chilkoot Pass in one

George Carmack

THE GOLD?

trip. In the Chinook language, *skookum* means "strong." These writers say that Skookum Jim went to the Klondike with Carmack to look for gold. But Skookum Jim's relatives remembered him differently. They knew him as Keish, a man who cared so much for his family that he traveled the Yukon looking for his sister, Kate, who had gone off to marry Carmack. They say Keish wasn't looking for gold. Whichever version is true, Skookum Jim spent the rest of his life looking for another gold strike. He never found one, but he saved his money, and when he died, he left it to his people. The Skookum Jim Friendship Centre in Whitehorse was built with Skookum Jim's money.

Skookum Jim

border between the two countries lay. So the North-West Mounted Police set up a post at the top of the Chilkoot Pass. At the post, the police told gold seekers they were on Canadian soil and collected taxes on any U.S. goods the adventurers carried.

The police also checked to make sure that each Stampeder had a year's worth of supplies. Everyday necessities would be hard to come by at the journey's end.

Most gold seekers had no experience backpacking heavy supplies up steep, icy slopes. They had to go up and down the trail many times to bring in all their equipment—sometimes on their hands and knees. So many gold seekers made the trip, that if climbers stopped to rest, it might be hours before they could get back in line.

During the gold rush in the Yukon, Stampeders struggled up the Chilkoot Pass in single file.

Climbers who made it to the Yukon then had to build boats to cross Lake Bennett. They traveled another 500 miles (804 km) down the Yukon River to Dawson City. Along the way, many gold seekers lost their boats, their supplies, and their lives.

For the first Stampeders, Dawson City wasn't really a city. It was a swamp. But as more prospectors arrived, the town grew quickly. Within a year, 4,000 newcomers had jammed into the town to camp in a jumble of tents amid mud and piles of supplies.

By 1898, at the height of the gold rush, 40,000 people had crowded into Dawson City. By this time, the community had fine restaurants and fancy hotels. Women wore the latest fashions from France, and Dawson City was nicknamed the Paris of the North.

As the Yukon's population rose, Canada earned a lot of tax money from the gold that was being panned and the liquor that was being sold in the region. So in 1898, the profitable Yukon became a separate Canadian territory with Dawson City as its capital.

To improve transportation to the new territory, a group of businesspeople planned the White Pass and Yukon Route Railway. Thousands of workers labored to punch a 110-mile (177-km) track through some of the steepest mountains in North America. Linking Skagway, Alaska, to Whitehorse, Yukon, the railroad opened in 1900. From Whitehorse, travelers could take steamboats in summer or horse-drawn sleighs in winter the rest of the way to Dawson City.

With the gold rush, life for First Nations people in the Yukon changed. Some Aboriginals began earning wages packing supplies for miners or cutting wood to fuel steamboats. Miners were hunting the game that Aboriginals depended on, so families had to travel farther to find food. Others moved from their traditional camps to escape the growing mining towns.

Mining the Miners

Thousands of people headed for the Klondike region of the Yukon in the late 1800s. Many of them came not to mine for gold but to "mine" the miners. In other words, they came to make their fortunes selling hard-to-get products—such as fruit, milk, eggs, newspapers, and bathtubs—to prospectors for huge profits. One businesswoman, Belinda Mulroney, toted $5,000 worth of silk, cotton, and hot-water bottles over the Chilkoot Pass. She sold the goods in Dawson City for $30,000, becoming one of the town's wealthiest residents.

Whitehorse, Yukon, (above) *became an important northern transportation hub after the completion of the White Pass and Yukon Route Railway in 1900. The new train line connected Whitehorse to Skagway, Alaska—an important ocean port.*

After the Gold Rush

In the early 1900s, the rich deposits of placer (river) gold ran out, and the gold rush ended as quickly as it had started. Although thousands of people had come to the Yukon, very few had struck it rich. By 1921 the population of the Yukon had dropped to about 4,000. The boom was over.

But other mines had opened in the Yukon by this time. Coal mines were operating at Carmacks, in southern Yukon. In central Yukon, lead, zinc, and silver mines employed workers in Mayo.

During World War II (1939–1945), the Yukon had another big rush. Plans to build new highways, airports, and oil pipelines for the war effort attracted about 30,000 people. Most of them were U.S. and Canadian military and construction workers.

As the Yukon developed in the 1900s, some First Nations people moved off their traditional lands to escape the crush of newcomers.

35

Army trucks cross a floating pontoon bridge over the Donjek River in southwestern Yukon. The bridge was one of hundreds built as part of the Alaska Highway.

One of these efforts was the Alaska Highway, which was built in 1942 and 1943 to move U.S. troops and supplies north to Alaska in case of an enemy attack by Japan. The 1,514-mile (2,436-km) gravel road passed through southwestern Yukon on its way from Dawson Creek, British Columbia, to Fairbanks, Alaska.

Some First Nations people worked in the Alaska Highway construction camps. After the road was completed, many Aboriginal families left their traditional homes on the land (away from settlements) and moved to the communities growing near the new road, which provided easier transportation than the old steamboats.

Workers began constructing the Canadian Oil (Canol) Project in 1942. More than 600 miles (965 km) long, the pipeline carried crude oil from Norman Wells, Northwest Territories, to a refinery in Whitehorse, Yukon. At the refinery, workers processed the oil into gasoline and other useful wartime oil products.

Just as most gold miners left the Yukon after the gold rush, most construction workers left the territory after the war. But some people liked the area and stayed.

Whitehorse flourished as a center for transportation, communication, and supplies. In 1953 the territory's capital was moved from Dawson City to Whitehorse. The new capital grew even more after 1964. That year miners discovered a huge lead and zinc de-

Since 1953 the capital of the Yukon has been in Whitehorse.

posit nearby, in what became the town of Faro.

The many groups who had come to the Yukon over the years brought new ways of doing things to the territory. Some of the new ways made life easier for Aboriginals, but other changes caused confusion, sickness, and even death.

One of the most difficult problems faced by Aboriginals was that they gradually lost control of their land and the power to govern themselves. Slowly, Aboriginals began working to get more control over their affairs. In 1973 a political organization called the Yukon Native Brotherhood, led by Elijah Smith, produced a document titled *Together Today for Our Children Tomorrow.* This booklet described Aboriginal claims to land in the Yukon.

First Nations people in the Yukon had never fought wars over land with newcomers. Nor had they signed **treaties** (agreements) with outsiders. The Aboriginals felt they still had a claim to the land they had lived on before non-Aboriginals arrived. Elijah Smith asked the Canadian government for compensation for all the land the Aboriginals had never officially given up. Land-claim negotiations began.

Almost 20 years later, in 1991, the governments of Canada and the Yukon signed an agreement with the Council for Yukon Indians. This political organization represents all 14 of the Yukon's First Nations bands.

The agreement gives a cash payment and about 9 percent of the Yukon to First Nations peoples. Each nation is in the process of selecting the land it wants and deciding when to take control of its own education, housing, and other responsibilities. By 1995 four of the First Nations had also signed agreements with the government to form their own local Aboriginal governments.

The Yukon is the first place in Canada to achieve this type of land-claim settlement. While the settlement speaks for many First Nations, it also allows individual bands to make their own decisions. Individual nations also can negotiate additional agreements with the government. Elijah Smith died in 1991, but his vision of helping tomorrow's children is truly alive.

In 1995 the Royal Canadian Mounted Police celebrated 100 years of service in the Yukon Territory.

Boom or Bust

The Yukon's economy is like a roller coaster. Ever since the gold rush, the territory's wealth and population have gone up and down. This "boom or bust" economy occurs partly because some towns depend on only one industry—mining.

When a town's mine is booming, the area attracts a lot of people. In a good year, for example, the territory earns almost half a billion dollars from mining. But when world prices for metals drop or the metal runs out, mines close and workers leave to find other jobs.

The biggest mine in the Yukon—the Grum lead and zinc deposit at Faro, which employed more than 500 people—closed in January of 1998. Mine owners plan to reopen a silver and lead mine near Elsa. Several other new mines are being developed to unearth hard-rock gold, copper, silver, and molybdenum—a metal often used to strengthen steel.

A giant steam shovel at a placer mine unloads gold-rich gravel into a sluice, where fast-running water separates small pieces of gold from the dirt.

A store cashier hands change to a customer. Cashiers and other service workers make up the majority of the Yukon's jobholders.

Gold mining is still important in the Yukon. Each summer as many as 1,000 people may work for mining companies, looking for placer gold, which is found among the sand and gravel of creeks and rivers. Placer gold is much easier to mine than gold embedded deep in hard rock. The Yukon also has supplies of oil and gas in the Arctic Ocean off the territory's northern coast. But the only operating gas plant is in southeastern Yukon. Altogether about 7 percent of the Yukon's workers have mining jobs.

The territory earns millions of dollars each year from tourism, which is part of the service industry. Rather than making products, workers with service jobs help other people. Service workers may be police officers, nurses, teachers, lawyers, politicians, truck drivers, salesclerks, or waiters. Most workers in the Yukon—about 81 percent—make a living from service jobs.

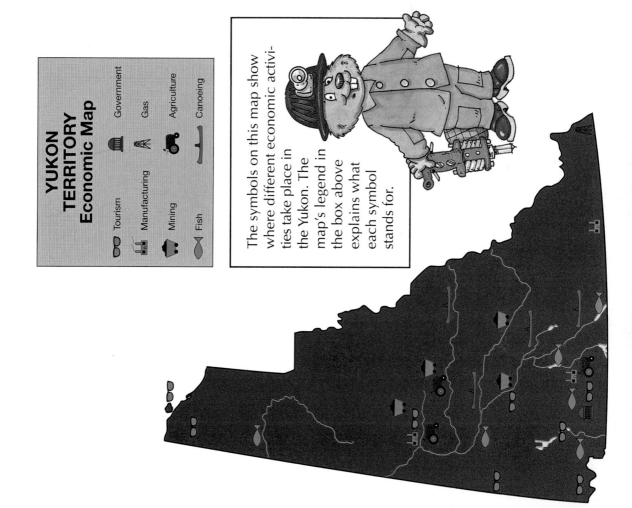

YUKON TERRITORY Economic Map

- 🕶 Tourism
- 🏭 Manufacturing
- ⛰ Mining
- 🐟 Fish
- 🏛 Government
- ⛽ Gas
- 🚜 Agriculture
- 🛶 Canoeing

The symbols on this map show where different economic activities take place in the Yukon. The map's legend in the box above explains what each symbol stands for.

Saving the Porcupine Caribou Herd

The large Porcupine Caribou Herd has over 160,000 barrenground caribou, who spend the winter in the Ogilvie and Richardson Mountains of north central Yukon. In the spring, the herd migrates north across the Porcupine River near Old Crow to the barrengrounds (Arctic plains) along the Arctic coast of the Yukon and the neighboring state of Alaska. Here, the caribou spend the summer bearing and raising their young.

Over the years, the caribou have been threatened by increased road construction, which brings more traffic and sports hunters to the animals' habitat, or wilderness home. New roads mean that the animals lose part of their habitat. And more hunters can lead to overhunting of the caribou. To protect caribou and their northern wilderness home, Ivvavik National Park and Vuntut National Park were created in northern Yukon. But the caribou herd faces another threat from just across the international border. The United States is considering oil exploration in Alaska's Arctic National Wildlife Refuge, which lies directly west of Ivvavik National Park.

Many people in both the United States and Canada fear the industrial activity will drive away or even destroy the Porcupine herd. And without the caribou—the main source of food and clothing for Aboriginal peoples in the area—the Aboriginals' way of life will be threatened.

Concerned citizens in the two countries are working to stop oil exploration in Alaska's Arctic National Wildlife Refuge. They hope that by preserving this wilderness area, both the Porcupine Caribou Herd and the local Aboriginal way of life will survive for generations to come.

About 2,000 service workers have jobs helping the 250,000 visitors who come to the Yukon each year. Some tourist workers have jobs as park rangers in Kluane National Park. Other workers guide fishers and hunters in the territory's many unspoiled wilderness areas. Expert rafters lead trips on the Yukon's scenic rivers. Pilots fly helicopters, taking skiers to the slopes of the Saint Elias Range.

Thousands of tourists visit the Yukon to celebrate a variety of landmark events. The 50th birthday of the Alaska Highway took place in 1992. Other celebrations include the 100th anniversary of the Yukon Territory and the gold rush in 1998 as well as the 100th birthday of the White Pass and Yukon Route Railway in the year 2000.

Stationed in Dawson City, these officers in the Department of Fisheries and Oceans work for the Canadian government.

Tourism and mining earn a lot of money for the Yukon, but government service jobs employ the most people. About 5,000 people in the Yukon work for the national, territorial, or city governments. They may be mayors, office managers, garbage collectors, engineers, or scientists.

Altogether, about 1 percent of working Yukoners have jobs in agriculture and fishing. Commercial fishers catch salmon on the Yukon River or raise arctic char at the fish farm in Whitehorse. But trapping and fishing are more important than just making money. They are also among the many ways that Aboriginals practice their culture. First Nations people in the Yukon return year after year to their traditional fish camps to net, spear, and dry salmon, trout, and whitefish.

Much of the soil in the Yukon is dry and infertile, and the growing season in the territory is very short—

Some Aboriginal fishers rely on the current of the Yukon River to turn fish wheels, which scoop up salmon and other fish swimming upstream to spawn (lay eggs).

Most farmers who grow crops in the Yukon plant oats and hay, which are used to feed livestock.

about three months. But the Yukon has more than 100 farms and some very enthusiastic farmers. They grow hay to feed horses and cattle. Grains include oats, wheat, and barley. Among the vegetable crops are potatoes, cabbages, tomatoes, cucumbers, and bean sprouts. Some farmers raise bees to produce honey, and some have sheep farms.

A few Yukoners raise bison and other animals on game farms.

Ranchers in the Yukon raise elk, bison, reindeer, and musk oxen for meat and hides. Some of the antlers are shipped to Asia, where they are ground up and used to manufacture medicines.

The Yukon's natural resources provide some of the territory's factory jobs. Laborers at the fish-processing plant in Dawson City freeze and can fish. Workers at sawmills near Watson Lake, Whitehorse, and Dawson City

Workers (left) *in Old Crow cut harvested trees into lumber. Some of the Yukon's lumber is used in local construction projects* (below).

cut wood from Yukon forests into lumber. Construction workers use the lumber to build offices and homes. About 10 percent of jobholders in the territory are employed in manufacturing and construction.

A Land of Legends and Traditions

At the height of the gold rush in 1898, more than 40,000 people lived in the Yukon. In 1998, 100 years later, only about 31,000 people called the territory home. About 75 percent of the Yukon's residents are non-Aboriginals. Most of these people can trace their roots to Great Britain, Germany, France, and other European countries.

Most Yukoners live in one of three towns—Whitehorse (the capital), Dawson City, or Watson Lake. About two-thirds of the territory's residents live in Whitehorse. The populations of the Yukon's other communities vary from less than 50 to a few hundred people. Although First Nations people make up only 25 percent of the territory's population, they are the majority in these smaller communities.

Two Yukoners work up a sweat in a sawing competition during the Yukon Sourdough Rendezvous.

With wilderness areas so close to everyone's backyard, it is no wonder that Yukoners love outdoor activities. The popular Yukon Quest—a 1,000-mile (1,609-km) dogsled race between Whitehorse and Fairbanks, Alaska—is probably one of the toughest races in the world. Following old wagon, sleigh, and mail routes, mushers must carry all their supplies and camp out in February's freezing weather, usually sleeping on their sleds.

In the old days, prospectors climbed the tough Chilkoot Pass to get from Alaska to the Yukon. Adventurous hikers still do. But nowadays a highway runs between Skagway, Alaska, and Whitehorse. Each summer, teams of runners compete on this 110-mile (177-km) road in an international road relay called the Klondike Trail of '98.

Participants in a cross-country ski race line up at the starting point.

Every two years, athletes from the Yukon compete with other northerners in the Arctic Winter Games. Because the main goal of the games is to make friends and learn about other cultures, the event is also known as the Friendly Games. Traditional Aboriginal games, such as the pole push, snow snake (javelin throw), and high kick, are played at the Friendly Games, as well as at the North American Indigenous Games. Schools in the Yukon are trying to encourage students to play these games so that Aboriginal cultures are not forgotten.

Students in a Whitehorse classroom play an Aboriginal game called stick gambling.

The most popular Aboriginal game in the territory is stick gambling. To participate, an even number of players sit facing each other. Each person has a little rock. The player changes the rock from hand to hand, trying to keep the opposing team from guessing which hand hides the rock. Sticks are used to keep track of points. The action is accompanied by drummers chanting songs.

The Yukon is proud of its many artists. You can find art by Yukoners in several galleries as well as on many of

Whitehorse's public buildings. The Yukon Arts Society, for example, painted large murals showing the history of the Alaska Highway and the work of the Royal Canadian Mounted Police. Other artists have sculptures and carvings on display in Whitehorse's many modern buildings.

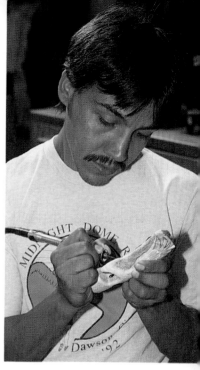

A Tlingit artist (left) *displays his carvings and painted ceremonial drums in Teslin. A Dawson City Gwich'in artist* (above) *carves a sculpture from an antler.*

Street musicians play the drums on Main Street in Whitehorse.

Music and dancing are important to Yukoners, too. Almost every First Nation has a group of dancers, singers, and musicians. The Nakai Theatre Ensemble is a professional theater company of Aboriginals and non-Aboriginals. The group presents original plays at the Yukon Arts Centre in Whitehorse and on tours to the territory's other communities.

First Nations women in the Yukon have long been known for their skillfully sewn jackets, mitts, and moccasins. Made out of tanned moose or caribou hides, the clothing is decorated with beads, fur, silk embroidery, or tufted moose hair. In addition, Yukon women are known for their decorated modern parkas.

Yukoners get together for many annual festivals. Each year in February, people have fun dressing themselves and their buildings in gold rush themes for the Yukon Sourdough Rendezvous in Whitehorse. They also take part in contests such as beard growing, flour packing, and poetry reciting. Discovery Days, which take place in Dawson City

Aboriginal drummers perform at a festival in Whitehorse.

each August, celebrate the discovery of gold in 1896. One of the highlights of the event is a lively parade staged by the Yukon's Order of Pioneers, a society of oldtimers from a variety of ethnic backgrounds.

Storytelling is a good way to bring people together, whatever their age or culture. On the last weekend in June every year, storytellers come to the Yukon from around the world. They gather in tents along the Yukon River in Whitehorse for what may be the largest and most unusual festival in the world—the Yukon International Storytelling Festival. Kids have their own tent shaped like a giant salmon and called the Nylon Zoo. Here, they can paint balloons, make masks, play games, and tell their own stories.

A crowd gathers to hear a reading of poems written by Robert Service, a famous author who lived in and wrote about the Yukon in the early 1900s.

Famous Yukoners

1 **Jerry Alfred** (born 1955) is an Aboriginal singer, drummer, guitarist, and storyteller whom elders have called Keeper of the Songs of the Northern Tutchone People. In 1994 he won the Aurora Award, which honors Yukon performing artists. Alfred lives in Pelly Crossing, Yukon.

2 **Laura** (1878–1967) and **Pierre Berton** (born 1920), mother and son, are writers known for their books about the Yukon. Laura, a Dawson City schoolteacher, wrote *I Married the Yukon*. Raised in Dawson City, Pierre wrote a famous book about the territory called *Klondike*.

Martha Louise Black (1866–1957), originally from Kansas, was one of the few women to hike over the Chilkoot Pass during the Yukon gold rush. She made the territory her home, and in 1936 became the Yukon's first woman—and Canada's second female—to be elected to the Canadian parliament.

Chris Caldwell (born 1958) moved to Whitehorse in the 1970s and became one of the territory's most popular artists. Her paintings, Christmas cards, and cartoons are inspired by the Yukon's mountains and wildlife.

5 **Charlie Peter Charlie, Sr.** (born 1919), is an Old Crow chief and band counselor from Johnson Creek, Yukon. He has helped record the language, history, and biology of northern Yukon. He is also a well-known fiddler.

6 **Ione Christensen** (born 1933) is a politician and writer from Fort Selkirk, Yukon. She has served as the mayor of Whitehorse and as the commissioner of the Yukon. She was the first woman to hold either of these positions and was appointed to the Order of Canada in 1994.

7 Judy Gingell (born 1946), a member and former manager of the Kwanlin Dun First Nation, was named the commissioner of the Yukon in 1995. Born on the land, Gingell served as chairperson of the Council for Yukon Indians from 1989 to 1995.

8 Leslie Hamson (born 1948) writes stories, poems, and newspaper articles but is best known for her plays. Many of her plays—including *Last Rites* and *Land(e)scapes*—have been staged at the Yukon Arts Centre in Whitehorse, where she lives.

■ **Ted Harrison** (born 1926), originally from England, moved to Whitehorse in 1968. He is well known for his brightly colored paintings of the Yukon, for which he has received many awards.

10 Rolf Hougen (born 1928), a Whitehorse businessperson, is a founder and a director of Canadian Satellite Communications, Inc., which provides television and radio service by satellite to isolated communities throughout Canada. Hougen also owns and operates The Hougen Centre—the largest retail operation in the Yukon.

11 Johnny Johns (1898–1988) of Carcross, Yukon, was one of North America's top hunting guides. He also guided engineers building the Alaska Highway and was a well-known singer, dancer, drummer, storyteller, and poet.

George Johnston (1884–1972) was a successful Tlingit trapper and noted photographer from Teslin, Yukon, who took pictures of the lifeway of his people between 1910 and 1940. Some of these photos are on display in Teslin at the George Johnston Museum, which is named after him.

Sam Johnston (born 1935), a Tlingit trapper from Teslin, is a clan leader, chief, and land-claims negotiator. With family members, he started the Teslin Tlingit Dancers in 1974 and went on to a political career, serving in the Yukon's legislative assembly from 1985 to 1992.

14 Edith Josie (born 1920) is a Gwich'in elder from Old Crow, Yukon. She is famous for "Here Are the News"—a newspaper column about daily life in this remote Aboriginal village in the Yukon's Arctic region. Published in the *Whitehorse Star,* Josie's stories of ordinary events such as hunting muskrat, picking berries, and playing tug-of-war won her the Order of Canada in 1995.

15 Audrey McLaughlin (born 1936) is the second woman in the Yukon to be elected to Canada's House of Commons, where she has served since 1987. She was also the first woman in Canada to lead a national political party, the New Democratic Party. McLaughlin lives in Whitehorse.

Jean-Marie Mouchet (born 1917) is a missionary from France who came to Old Crow in 1951 and began a skiing school for children, which is still in operation. One of the priest's first pupils, Martha Benjamin, was the first Yukoner to win a national skiing title.

■ **Dick North** (born 1929) is a writer who lives in Whitehorse. Two of his most famous books are *The Mad Trapper of Rat River* and *The Lost Patrol.*

18 **Louise Profeit-LeBlanc** (born 1951) is a descendant of Northern Tutchone people and has spent much of her life promoting her culture. She is a founding member of the Yukon's International Storytelling Festival and is the Native heritage adviser for the Yukon Department of Tourism. Profeit-LeBlanc lives in Whitehorse.

■ **Jim Robb** (born 1933) is an illustrator, writer, and photographer who lives in Whitehorse. He is best known for *The Colourful Five Per Cent Illustrated,* a magazine series and book featuring drawings and stories about unusual people and buildings in the Yukon.

■ **Angela Sidney** (1902–1991) was one of the last speakers and teachers of the Tagish language. With the help of an anthropologist, she recorded and published the songs, stories, and traditions of her people in books such as *Life Lived Like a Story* and *My Stories Are My Wealth.* From Tagish, Yukon, she was awarded the Order of Canada in 1985.

21 **Elijah Smith** (1912–1991) was a Southern Tutchone elder and chief of the Kwanlin Dun Band in Whitehorse. As the first president of the Yukon Native Brotherhood, he published *Together Today for Our Children Tomorrow*—a document about Aboriginal land claims in the Yukon.

22 **Florence Whyard** (born 1917) is an author, publisher, and politician. A longtime resident of Whitehorse, she has served as the city's mayor, as a cabinet minister in the Yukon's legislative assembly, and as the administrator for the territory. Whyard also publishes history books for children.

Fast Facts

Territorial Symbols

Flower: fireweed

Bird: raven

Tartan: blue for glacier-fed waters and mountain skies, magenta for the fireweed floral emblem, green for forests, purple for mountains in the northern sky, white for winter snow, and yellow for gold and midnight sun evenings.

Territorial Highlights

Landmarks: Herschel Island, Chilkoot Trail, Kluane National Park, White Pass and Yukon Route Railway in Whitehorse, S.S. *Klondike* in Whitehorse, MacBride Museum and Yukon Arts Centre in Whitehorse, Robert Service Cabin in Dawson City, Dawson City Museum in Dawson City, George Johnston Museum in Teslin, Fort Selkirk near Minto, Carcross Desert near Carcross

Annual events: Southern Lakes Dogsled Race in Carcross (Jan.), Frostbite Music Festival in Whitehorse (Feb.), Alsek Music Festival in Haines Junction (June), Dun Na Kwe Ye (People Celebrating) in Whitehorse (June), Shortest Night in Burwash Landing (June), Dawson City Music Festival (July), Dena Cultural Exchange in Ross River (July), Yukon Gold Panning Championships in Dawson City (July), Discovery Days in Watson Lake (Aug.)

Population

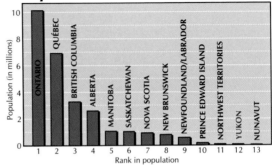

Population*: 30, 766

Rank in population, nationwide: 12th

Population distribution: 60 percent urban; 40 percent rural

Population density: 0.3 people per sq mi (0.1 per sq km)

Capital: Whitehorse (19,157)

Towns and villages (and populations*): Dawson City (1, 287), Faro (1, 261), Watson Lake (993), Haines Junction (574), Carmacks (466), Mayo (324), Teslin (189)

Major ethnic groups*: British, 19 percent; Aboriginal peoples, 14 percent; German, 4 percent; French, 3 percent; Scandinavian, 2 percent; Dutch, Italian, Ukrainian, 1 percent each; other backgrounds, 55 percent

*1996 census

Endangered and Threatened Species

Mammals: wood bison
Birds: anatum peregrine falcon

Geographic Highlights

Area (land/water): 186,660 sq mi (483,450 sq km)
Rank in area, nationwide: 9th
Highest point: Mount Logan (19,550 ft/5,959 m)
Major rivers: Yukon, Pelly, Stewart, Teslin, Klondike, Peel, Porcupine, Macmillan
Major lakes: Teslin, Tagish, Kluane, Laberge, Kusawa, Aishihik, Bennett

Economy
Percentage of Workers Per Job Sector

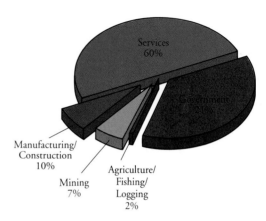

Services 60%

Government 21%

Manufacturing/
Construction
10%

Mining
7%

Agriculture/
Fishing/
Logging
2%

Natural resources: asbestos, coal, copper, gold, lead, nickel, silver, zinc, molybdenum, forests, water
Agricultural products: hay, oats, wheat, barley, potatoes, cabbages, bean sprouts, honey, elk, bison, musk oxen
Manufactured goods: lumber and wood products, printed materials, food products, clothing

Energy

Electric power: hydropower (86 percent), diesel fuel (14 percent)

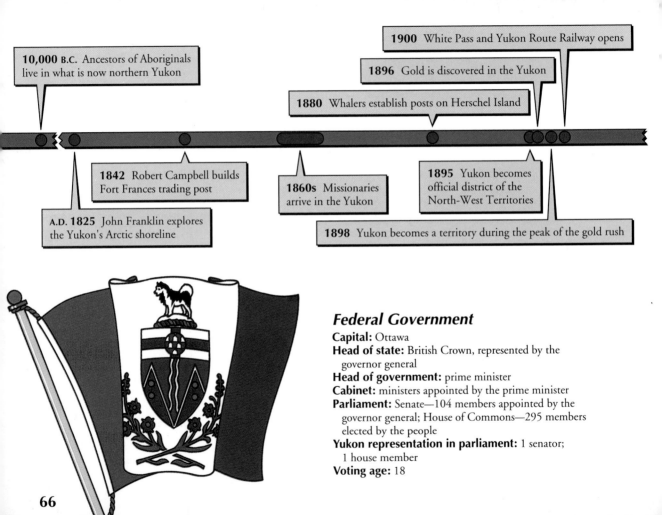

1900 White Pass and Yukon Route Railway opens

1896 Gold is discovered in the Yukon

10,000 B.C. Ancestors of Aboriginals live in what is now northern Yukon

1880 Whalers establish posts on Herschel Island

1842 Robert Campbell builds Fort Frances trading post

1860s Missionaries arrive in the Yukon

1895 Yukon becomes official district of the North-West Territories

A.D. 1825 John Franklin explores the Yukon's Arctic shoreline

1898 Yukon becomes a territory during the peak of the gold rush

Federal Government

Capital: Ottawa
Head of state: British Crown, represented by the
  governor general
Head of government: prime minister
Cabinet: ministers appointed by the prime minister
Parliament: Senate—104 members appointed by the
  governor general; House of Commons—295 members
  elected by the people
Yukon representation in parliament: 1 senator;
  1 house member
Voting age: 18

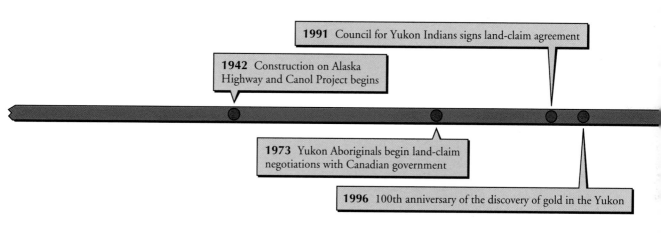

1991 Council for Yukon Indians signs land-claim agreement

1942 Construction on Alaska Highway and Canol Project begins

1973 Yukon Aboriginals begin land-claim negotiations with Canadian government

1996 100th anniversary of the discovery of gold in the Yukon

Territorial Government

Capital: Whitehorse
Head of state: commissioner
Head of government: government leader
Cabinet: 6 members chosen by the government leader
from the Legislative Assembly
Legislative Assembly: 17 members
Voting age: 18
Major political parties: Yukon, New Democratic,
Liberal, Independent Alliance

Government Services

To help pay the people who work for the Yukon's government, the people of the Yukon pay taxes on money they earn and on many of the items they buy. The services run by the territorial government help assure the people of the Yukon a high quality of life. Government funds pay for medical care, for education, for road building and repairs, and for other facilities such as libraries and parks. In addition, the government has funds to help people who are disabled, elderly, or poor.

Glossary

cordillera A group of mountain ranges, usually the main mountain group of a continent or region. The western Cordillera of North America, for example, includes many ranges, such as the Rockies and the Sierra Nevada. The term *cordillera* comes from a Spanish word meaning "chain."

glacier A large body of ice and snow that flows down mountain valleys, often following paths originally formed by rivers. The term is also used to refer to masses of ice that move slowly over the land's surface.

ice age A period when ice covers large regions of the earth's surface. The term *Ice Age* usually refers to the most recent one, called the Pleistocene, which began almost 2 million years ago and ended about 10,000 years ago.

missionary A person sent out by a religious group to spread its beliefs to other people.

permafrost Ground that remains permanently frozen. A shallow layer of surface soil may thaw during the summer, but the ground below does not.

plateau   A large, relatively flat area that stands above the surrounding land.

precipitation   Rain, snow, and other forms of moisture that fall to earth.

treaty   An agreement between two or more groups, usually having to do with peace or trade.

Pronunciation Guide

Aboriginal (a-buh-RIH-juh-nuhl)

Athapascan (a-thuh-PAS-kuhn)

Beaufort Sea (BOH-fuhrt)

Chilkoot (CHIHL-koot)

Cordillera (kawhr-duhl-YEHR-uh)

Gwich'in (GWIH-chuhn)

Han (HAHN)

Herschel (HUHR-shuhl)

Kaska (KAS-kuh)

Kluane (kloo-AH-nee)

Ogilvie (OH-guhl-vee)

Selwyn (SEHL-wihn)

Tagish (TA-gihsh)

Tanana (TA-nuh-nuh)

Tlingit (KLING-kuht)

Tutchone (tuh-SHOH-nee)

Yukon (YOO-kahn)

Index

About the Author

Lyn Hancock, originally from Australia, has lived in and traveled throughout the Canadian North since 1972. She started her career as an elementary and high-school teacher and is now an award-winning photographer, lecturer, and writer whose books include *There's a Seal in My Sleeping Bag* and *Nunavut,* a Lerner "Hello Canada" title. Ms. Hancock currently lives in Lantzville, British Columbia.

Acknowledgments

Laura Westlund, pp. 1, 3, 64, 65 (right), 66-67; Terry Boles, pp. 6, 12, 43, 65; Mapping Specialists Ltd., pp. 12-13, 43; © Beth Davidow, pp. 2, 7, 8 (inset), 9, 15 (top), 17 (right), 19, 20, 21, 37, 41, 42, 44, 45, 46, 49 (right), 55 (both), 59 (inset right), 71; Elaine Wadsworth, p. 8; Jenny Hager/Alpine Images, p. 11; David Dvorak, Jr., p. 14; Peter Langer/Associated Media Group, pp. 15 (bottom), 16, 20 (inset), 50, 56, 58, 59; Darielle Talarico, p. 18; Artwork by John Erste, pp. 23, 25; Canadian Museum of Civilization, #K75-944, p. 24; National Archives of Canada, pp. 26 (C-2263), 34 (PA-48318); Denver Public Library, Western History Department, p. 27; Jesuit Oregon Province Archives, Gonzaga University, p. 28 (JOPA 104.01); North Wind Picture Archives, p. 29; Yukon Archives, pp. 30 (Alaska Historical Library Coll. #4160), 31 (Oral History Coll. 88/58 #34), 32 (E. A. Hegg Coll. #2492), 35 (C. Tidd Coll. #7533), 36 (McBride Museum Coll. #3554); Royal Canadian Mounted Police, p. 39; Yukon Government, p. 47; © Lyn Hancock, pp. 48, 49 (left), 52, 53, 54, 57, 59 (inset left and inset center), 60 (top right), 61 (bottom left), 62 (top right), 69; Paul Casselman, p. 60 (far left); Cameras North, p. 60 (center); Rene'e Frost, p. 60 (bottom right); Office of the Commissioner of Yukon, p. 61 (top left); Marten Berkman, p. 61 (top right); Williams Bros. Photographers Ltd., p. 61 (center); New Democratic Party, p. 62 (bottom left); Renate Schmidt, p. 63 (top right); Council of Yukon First Nations, p. 63 (center left); James Whyard, p. 63 (bottom right); Steve Warble/Mountain Magic, p. 68.

971.91
H

Ville de Montréal

**Feuillet
de circulation**

À rendre le	
⊮ - DEC 1998	
Z 2 2 JAN '99	
Z 06 MAR '99	

06.03.375-8 (05-93)